Spiritual Exercises
for Church Leaders

Facilitator's Guide

Spiritual Exercises for Church Leaders

Dolores R. Leckey
and
Paula Minaert

Facilitator's Guide

A Project of the
Woodstock Theological Center

PAULIST PRESS
New York • Mahwah, N.J.

Cover design by Valerie Petro
Book design by ediType

Illustrations copyright © 2003 by Stephen Titra

Copyright © 2003 by The Woodstock Theological Center

Library of Congress Cataloging-in-Publication Data

Leckey, Dolores R.
    Spiritual exercises for church leaders : facilitator's guide / Dolores R. Leckey, Paula Minaert.
        p. cm.
    "A project of the Woodstock Theological Center."
    ISBN 0-8091-4095-0
    1. Christian leadership–Catholic Church. 2. Spiritual exercises. I. Minaert, Paula. II. Title.
    BX1803 .L43 2003
    248.8′9–dc21

                                                                2002156421

Published by Paulist Press
997 Macarthur Boulevard
Mahwah, New Jersey 07430

www.paulistpress.com

Printed and bound in the
United States of America

Contents

Foreword

Spirituality —
A Pearl of Great Price

In his classic *Markings,* Dag Hammarskjöld (1905–1961), former secretary general of the United Nations, expressed a deep spiritual longing: "If only I may grow: firmer, simpler — quieter, warmer."[1]

Hammarskjöld was a political leader, one who served the common good and fostered world peace. In his spiritual journal he records little of his political involvement but centers on his relationship with God and how that relationship impacted the rest of his life. Journaling was for him a spiritual exercise of utmost importance, fostering a sense of clarity, depth, and continuity.

All of us who are called to be leaders — be it in the Church, our homes, or society at large, have a need to grow firmer in our convictions, simpler in our lifestyle, quieter in the interior of our hearts, warmer in our relationships. We grow through exercising our spiritual faculties of knowing and loving, of imaging and remembering, of pondering and deciding. In *Spiritual Exercises for Church Leaders* we are given a vision and a methodology for ongoing personal and communal development. This work incorporates the insights and practical wisdom of two great teachers: St. Ignatius of Loyola and Bernard Lonergan. Here is a book that takes us into the mystery of the human person and offers ways in which we might

7

live more effectively the call to be truly human, truly disciples of the Lord Jesus.

Spirituality is about growth, developing our potential in reference to God and how that life in God impacts all the other aspects of our life: the social, the political, the cultural, the economic. Three major calls comprise our spiritual journey: the call to listen attentively, the call to respond wholeheartedly, the call to participate fully.

To listen attentively. The French philosopher Simone Weil held the conviction that *attention* is central both to a Christian conception of studies and the command to love. She writes: "Not only does the love of God have attention for its substance; the love of our neighbor, which we know to be the same love, is made of this same substance."[2] In an age suffering from the malady of inattentiveness, our challenge is to be open to the divine speech. God speaks to us through everyday experiences, the intuitions of the heart, the legacy of our rich Christian tradition, the Bible. Two requirements on our part: a radical openness and a deep interior silence. To be human is to hear. Other voices seek our attention: the radio and television, the roar of the madding crowd, our own interior Grand Central Station. The din and cacophony can be overwhelming. Yet God not only speaks to us but offers the Holy Spirit to dwell within us to help us discern the action of divine grace. With Jesus as mentor and model we have a message and a lifestyle that help us to sort out what is of God — light, love, life — and what is not — darkness, indifference, and death.

To respond wholeheartedly. Listening is one side of the coin, loving is the other. The Carmelite poet Jessica Powers maintained that to live with the Spirit of God embraced two things: being a listener and being a lover. Our hearing of God's word — to feed the hungry, to forgive sins seventy times seven times, to carry one another's burdens — is to be followed by a wholehearted response. Nonresponsiveness, like inattentiveness, is death to spirituality.

St. Thérèse of Lisieux, affectionately known as the Little Flower, was a responder to God's call. She saw her vocation as a call to love, to be love, to make Love loved. Though she lived only twenty-four years, she lived a full life. This Doctor of the Church models for us someone who lived intensely the Ignatian process of loving attention, one who explored and discerned, one who acted with great responsibility, one who treasured not only her own community but through missionary zeal, the whole Church.

To participate fully. An old adage: "Growth demands participation." We are not here on earth to be observers, watching life pass us by. We are to enter in, tasting the joys and sorrows of life, experiencing victories and defeats, sharing good and tough times. Spirituality is a full participation in the paschal mystery.

Robert Ellsberg, in his book *All Saints,* gives a brief summary of the life and ministry of 365 individuals who refused the role of observer and committed themselves to participate fully in the vocation God assigned to them. We are told about the great saints such as Augustine of Hippo and Teresa of Avila; we hear about the Hindu "saint" Gandhi, who led his country to freedom and independence; we are shown the dedication of Dorothy Day and her Catholic Worker movement as well as Dietrich Bonhoeffer, who boldly stated the cost of discipleship. These people, all leaders in their various areas, emphasized the importance of spiritual discipline if they were to grow in justice and holiness. Listening, exploring, discerning, responding — markings that led them and their people to fullness of life.

Spiritual Exercises for Church Leaders is theological and practical. It offers a perspective on human existence and a methodology proven in its development of human potential. Its value lies in its participatory style, its clarity of purpose, its realism. While highly pragmatic, it also contains a depth that leads to transformation.

In the Second Vatican Council document *Lumen Gentium,* the Dogmatic Constitution on the Church, we are reminded that our universal call is to holiness. Our vocation is to sanctity. *Spiritual Exercises for Church Leaders* is intended to be a helpful resource in responding to the call. It is clear from the text that our response is both a matter of grace and serious human work. Further, this call to holiness is neither romantic nor remote. The poet Gordon Gilsdorf captures well the essence of sanctity:

A SAINT

We look
for mystic gold
and silvered ecstasy
and find a tempered, twisted piece
of steel.[3]

Robert F. Morneau
Auxiliary Bishop
Green Bay, Wisconsin

Notes

    1. Dag Hammarskjöld, *Markings,* trans. Leif Sjoberg and W. H. Auden (New York: Alfred A. Knopf, 1981), 93.

    2. "Reflections on the Right Use of School Studies with a View to the Love of God," in *The Simone Weil Reader,* ed. George A. Panichas (New York: David MacKay, 1977), 51.

    3. Gordon Gilsdorf, *The Same Five Notes* (Francestown, N.H.: Golden Quill Press, 1967), 93.

Acknowledgments

This book is based on a vision that gave rise to the Woodstock Church Leadership Program, inaugurated in 1996 with the financial support of the Raskob Foundation for Catholic Activities. The former director of the Woodstock Theological Center, James L. Connor, S.J., was convinced of the urgent need for the Catholic Church in the United States to respond intelligently, imaginatively, and courageously to the many challenges that rapid change was and is engendering in the culture. He and Msgr. Richard Liddy, a Woodstock fellow (now on the faculty of Seton Hall University), developed a retreat/workshop format to address this need. Select groups of church leaders came together to reflect, in a prayerful atmosphere, on their experiences of leadership in the contemporary Church and to seek a deeper understanding of the kind of leadership Jesus Christ desires for the Church. One clear direction emerged from the seven leadership workshops: namely, the need for commitment to a collaborative model of ministry, both within the Catholic Church (clergy/lay, men/women) and beyond it to collaboration with other churches and community organizations.

During the three years of workshops, a number of Woodstock fellows and associates served as presenters and helped to sharpen the program: Rev. Raymond Kemp, Edmundo Rodriguez, S.J., Thomas J. Reese, S.J., Dr. J. Michael Stebbins, and, of course, James Connor and Richard Liddy. Their pioneering work is evident everywhere in this project.

We saw the book as a necessary next step to allow for a wider church population to benefit from what was learned during those experimental years. The task of transforming lectures and group dynamics into reflective material for individuals and groups, while faithfully conveying the teachings of St. Ignatius and the methodology of Bernard Lonergan, was enormously helped by Michael Stebbins's expertise in these matters. I thank him for his generous gift of time. The interpretation of Lonergan's method, however, is that of the authors. Commentaries on the passages in the Acts of the Apostles (in the Facilitator's Guide) are the contributions of Fr. Edmundo Rodriguez, S.J., who, in turn, is indebted to the insights of Scripture scholar Luke Timothy Johnson.

Brother Dunstan Robidoux, O.S.B., graciously welcomed us to the Lonergan Institute on the grounds of St. Anselm's Abbey in Washington, D.C., so that we could work on the text in the atmosphere of monastic quietude. His own interest in Lonergan, combined with Benedictine hospitality, blessed our work in many ways.

As the text developed, we wanted to see if, indeed, it would be beneficial to a wide variety of leadership groups. Again, with financial support from the Raskob Foundation we were able to field test the materials and fine tune our book. I am deeply grateful to Edmund Gordon, secretary for Christian Formation, Diocese of Wilmington; Helen Lynch Byrnes, pastoral staff, Miraculous Medal Parish, Long Island; Rev. David McDonald, pastor of Blessed Sacrament Parish in Hamden, Connecticut; Robert Moriarty, S.M., coordinator for Small Christian Communities, Archdiocese of Hartford; and Horace Grinnell, pastor of St. Anthony's Parish in Falls Church, Virginia. All of them led leadership groups, met with Woodstock fellows and staff, offered suggestions and directions, and significantly influenced the development of the project. Two other groups, one in New Mexico led by Russell Raskob and another at St. Anselm's Abbey, co-led by the authors (with assistance from Brother Dunstan Robidoux, O.S.B.), provided valuable insights into how effective this particular vision of church leadership can be in a variety of settings.

Words of gratitude are certainly due to the priests, lay leaders, bishops, and religious who participated in the original workshops as Woodstock sought "to get it right." They provided affirmation and critique (both in ample measure) and urged us to continue to share the vision in some way. That's why *Spiritual Exercises for Church Leaders* was produced, and their wisdom is really on every page.

Collaboration, while worthwhile and even necessary, is rarely easy. Collaboration in writing a book can be particularly taxing. In this case, however, working with Paula Minaert has been not only exciting; it has been enlightening. She has the gift of taking complex ideas and making them come alive in story and metaphor. Her love of God and her love for the Church have made this work, and our working together, more beatitude than tribulation.

Finally, invaluable technical assistance, at various stages of the project, was ably and willingly provided by Maria Ferrara, administrative assistant at the Woodstock Center. She lightened our burden considerably.

Dolores R. Leckey
Coordinator
Church Leadership Program
Woodstock Theological Center

Introduction

Spiritual Exercises for Church Leaders grows out of the Church Leadership Program of the Woodstock Theological Center, which designed a systematic approach to the development of authentic leadership within the Church. The approach was field tested in a number of different settings over the course of a seven-year period. This book now intends to extend the arc of learning to a much wider audience. It is a handbook, a guide, for *all* church leaders — clergy, lay, and religious — as they work to serve the Church faithfully and effectively in the contemporary world.

These exercises, both the content and the process, begin with a focus on gratitude, the foundation of spiritual growth. They then move through the steps needed for authentic leadership: being attentive and intelligent, being discerning and responsible. These are the steps that lead to conversion and ultimately to authenticity. The reader, whether working alone or in a group, is encouraged to go deeply into this process.

The spiritual insights of St. Ignatius of Loyola and the theological method of Bernard Lonergan are integral parts of this process. So is Scripture. In particular, certain passages from the Acts of the Apostles show how leadership developed in the early church, and how we can learn from that experience. Other disciplines — the arts, history, and sociology — and reflective exercises are resources for understanding how change occurs, how culture impacts our religious understanding, and how creative solutions to contemporary problems can be fostered.

Goals

The specific goals of this process are listed briefly both in this book (page 22–23) and in the Participant's Book (page 22). But let's look at them here as well.

The first goal is to help participants *be attentive in a new way to their experience of themselves as church leaders*. This is based on the fact that personal experience allows us to know what is real, what is true, what is good. Knowledge can be gained directly; it does not have to be secondhand.

The second goal is to help participants *understand themselves, their communities, the Church, and the world in the context of God's redemptive presence in human history*. This goal puts our personal experience within the context of our Catholic Christian belief. We assume that God is acting, and has always acted, in our lives, in the lives of others, and in the world around us. The reality that we are trying to understand is essentially relational: we are related to God and to each other.

The third goal is to help participants *understand the dynamism of human consciousness as essential to authentic church leadership*. This dynamism is how we human beings work. Understanding it allows us to make sense of our experience, both as individuals and as leaders within our communities. Being faithful to it enables us to see and follow God acting in our lives and in our communities.

The fourth goal is to help participants *become more adept at discerning the particular ways in which God is calling them and their communities to live lives of discipleship*. As we practice being attentive to this dynamic, God-given movement within ourselves, we better understand God's call to us and to our communities.

All of these goals are designed to enable church leaders to make good decisions.

The Role of Facilitator

Your role as facilitator is to help open this small group, this microcosm of community, to the action of the Holy Spirit. You will guide them through a process that begins with gratitude to God—the foundation of spiritual growth, as we noted above — and then explores the dynamism of human consciousness, to which we refer in the goals. The four aspects, or capacities, of this dynamism are attentiveness, exploration, discernment, and responsibility. And, as people go through these different aspects on their ongoing journey to God, they find that they have been changed. They experience conversion.

The material in this book is designed to help the participants in your group reflect deeply on these matters. It uses Scripture, examples from history and current events, and various types of exercises to do this. Specifically, it uses Ignatian meditation and the Examen, because we believe that they are tried and tested methods for spiritual growth. The content of the sessions, the exercises based on them, and the "homework" are all meant to evoke the dynamism of consciousness within the participants. They become new spiritual exercises, inspired by those of Ignatius.

We explore passages from the Acts of the Apostles in each session. Despite the fact that many aspects of the Church seem new, especially since Vatican II, church leaders have always faced many of the same issues. The passages selected show how leadership developed in the early church — and how we can learn from that early experience.

This book, then, is an invitation to dialogue. The Woodstock Theological Center welcomes your reaction.

Practical Guidelines

1. If it is possible, give all the group members their Participant's Book ahead of time. Ask them to read the Overview (pages 15–23) before the first session. This is the preferred method of starting. Tell them they will need to bring the Participant's Book with them to each session.

2. Be sure to read the material for each session (in both this Facilitator's Guide and the Participant's Book) beforehand. There is usually something in each session that you have to think about and prepare before the meeting. For example, you will need to gather materials (photos, pictures, music, etc.) to put together the presentation on gratitude in Session One. For most of the sessions, you will need to have newsprint, markers, and tape as well. At the last session, a Eucharist will be held, so you will need to make all the arrangements for that.

3. You can adjust the times suggested in this book. Depending on the size of your group, you can either lengthen or shorten your meeting time or spend more time with one activity than with others. Do what works best for your group.

4. You may find it helpful to sit down after each session and jot down your thoughts about the meeting. What went well? What did people find hard to do? What might have worked better? Did you adapt the format to meet

your group's needs, and if so, how? Doing this while the meeting is still fresh in your mind will make it easier. It will also help you in your evaluations.

5. In Session Six, the group will be discussing and brainstorming solutions for some issue in your community. It would be helpful to pay attention during the earlier meetings and note what issues engage people. What concerns them? Don't decide after just one or two sessions; just be aware. This will give you information that will help you choose the issue, which you will present to the group at the end of Session Five.

6. Once you have gathered a group together, we recommend that you not add new people after the sessions have begun. The sessions — the exercises, the readings, the presentations — all build on each other, and it would be difficult for anyone coming in late.

Note: For each session, be sure to:

- set up the meeting space beforehand
- pray to the Holy Spirit for guidance and discernment before the meeting begins
- greet people as they arrive and give them name tags
- start on time
- begin with a prayer, which you or a member of the group can say

Session One

Gratitude

I. Welcome and Introductions (20 minutes)

1. Welcome everyone to Spiritual Exercises for Church Leaders. Say a little bit about who you are and why you agreed to lead this group.

2. Have participants introduce themselves. Say something like:

   Before we start the seminar itself and talk about what we hope to do here, let's learn something about each other.

   Ask people to give their names, why they're there, and one fact about themselves they'd like to share with the group.

II. Scripture Passage (5 minutes)
Deuteronomy 30:11–14
THE NEARNESS OF GOD

Surely, this commandment that I am commanding you today is not too hard for you, nor is it too far away. It is not in heaven, that you should say, "Who will go up to heaven for us, and get it for us so that we may hear it and observe it?" Neither is it beyond the sea, that you should say, "Who will cross to the other side of the sea for us, and get it for us so that we may hear it and observe it?" No, the word is very near to you; it is in your mouth and in your heart for you to observe.

1. Ask one person to read out loud the passage from Deuteronomy (page 25 in the Participant's Book). Explain that the group will reflect on it in silence afterward.

2. After the passage is read, allow two or three minutes of quiet.

III. Goals and Overview of the Seminar (10 minutes)

1. Transition to talking about the goals. Say something like:

   > *With these words, Moses is trying to tell the Israelites how to follow God's ways, how to discern God's will. In addition to the teachings that have been handed down, look within; what you need to know is there. God is close to you, right next to you. This is not just a fanciful image. Moses is describing a fundamental human reality, one that is just as true today as it was then. To learn about God and his will for us, we need only look at ourselves and how we work, because God has woven his will into our very beings. It is this understanding that lies behind the goals of this seminar.*

   Go over the goals, which are on page 22 of the Participant's Book.

   ### Goals of the Seminar
   To help participants . . .

   - be attentive in a new way to their experience of themselves as church leaders;

- understand themselves, their communities, the Church, and the world in the context of God's redemptive presence in human history;

- understand the dynamism of human consciousness as essential to authentic church leadership;

- become more adept at discerning the particular ways in which God is calling them and their communities to live lives of discipleship.

2. Then, using the table of contents in the Participant's Book, go over the overall content of the seminar with the group. Explain the sequence of the six sessions.

3. Point out that the seminar's goals are not simple or easy. It will take work to move toward them. Discuss the importance of the participants' commitment to attending the sessions and working with the material between the sessions. The whole seminar is rooted in the participants' experience and will be fruitful for them to the extent that they allow what they learn at the sessions to touch their lives outside the sessions.

4. Tell the participants that this first session will contain an overview; an introduction to the Examen of Ignatius; a presentation on gratitude; an individual exercise and a group activity; a look at the assignments for the next session; and a closing prayer. Subsequent sessions will use the following format:

- Opening Prayer

- Scripture Processing. The passage will have been assigned the week before.

- Presentation by the Facilitator

- Exercise/Activity. This may happen individually, in pairs or small groups, or as a whole group. There are work pages for these activities.

- Assignments are given for the next session: the Scripture passage, other readings, etc.

- Closing Prayer

5. Ask if there are any questions.

IV. Preliminary Remarks (10 minutes)

1. Talk about the concepts in the Overview, which is found on pages 15–23 of the Participant's Book. Begin by saying something like:

   I want to know what you think are the biggest problems facing the Church today. In one or two words, can you tell me your opinions?

   On a piece of newsprint, write down what people say. Various things may come up: decline in vocations, divorce, low Mass attendance, liturgies too formal, liturgies too casual, how to integrate different ethnic groups, etc. Be careful — you want short answers, not monologues.

2. Mention how some problems in the Church have been so bitter that they have resulted in parishes breaking apart, dioceses on the verge of bankruptcy, and lasting ruptures between individuals and groups. Refer to the example from New York State mentioned in the Participant's Book (page 16).

3. Then introduce the idea that, even though we may think the Church has never had to deal with difficulties before,

history tells us otherwise. Talk about the other example in the Participant's Book, the one from the twelfth century (page 17). Add other examples if you wish, if there is time. Stress that the Church has rarely been totally free from dissension and conflict. It is alive and changing, not an unmoving monolith.

4. Add that this has been especially obvious since the Second Vatican Council, when the Church, and we as church leaders, realized that we need to understand and respond to today's world and today's culture — while still being loyal to the Church.

V. Presentation: The Examen (10 minutes)

1. *Note:* Please read the Overview in the Participant's Book (pages 15–23) for background and information about Ignatius and the Examen. Then, in presenting the Examen, transition by saying something like: "There is one particular tool that for many years has been very fruitful for people. It provides a way for us to try to discern God's will for us as individuals. It also helps us discern God's call to us within the Church and the world. This is the Ignatian Examen."

2. Briefly describe the five steps of the Examen, which are also listed on page 22–23 of the Participant's Book:

   • Become quiet and try to be aware of God's presence. Give God thanks for his great love for you.

   • Ask God for the insight to see the Holy Spirit acting in your life and for the grace to understand and respond to the divine call.

- Recall in your mind a specific segment of time — a day, half-day, week, etc. Look for instances of God's presence in your life. These could be desires, fears, memories, etc. What has been happening? How did you respond? Is there a pattern?

- Evaluate what happened in this slice of time and your response to what happened. How did you cooperate with God and God's call? Give thanks for these occasions. How did you not cooperate? Ask pardon for these occasions.

- Plan how you will collaborate more effectively with God as he acts in your life. Specifically, what do you need to do for this to happen? Prepare to carry it out. Pray for the grace to do it. Close with an Our Father.

3. Tell people you will be returning to the Examen later in the seminar.

VI. Presentation: Gratitude (20 minutes)

1. Suggestion: Start by showing, not telling. Before the session, gather together anything you can think of that might inspire gratitude in people. You can collect photographs and magazine pictures of children, families, food, beautiful scenes from nature, animals, cityscapes, works of art, churches, people helping people, etc. If you have the resources, you can show slides or play music that you think might appeal to the members of the group. Take into account people's ages and racial and ethnic makeup, too, as well as the history of your particular region, city, and parish. What would be meaningful to your audience?

2. Discuss gratitude. You may want to use the following essay for information and ideas.

GRATITUDE

The word "gratitude" comes from the Latin word *gratus,* which meant grateful or pleasing. *Gratus* is also akin to a Sanskrit word that translates as "he praises." Our word "grace" — meaning unmerited divine assistance given to humans for their sanctification — also comes from *gratus.*

The etymology reflects a profound reality: gratitude is related to grace. It's our gratitude and God's grace. The one flows from the other, is a response to it. We are grateful for God's grace. We praise God for it.

Gratitude forms the bookends of this short course. You will notice in the Examen that Ignatius begins with the simple instruction to give thanks. Be grateful, he says. Why? This doesn't seem to make sense. After all, we are undertaking this seminar, these spiritual exercises, because we feel a lack. Things are not as they should be. *We* are not as we should be. We are trying to correct flaws and solve problems, to change things, with God's help. This is serious business. But nothing has happened yet, so why give thanks?

This attitude misses a profound understanding that Ignatius had, an understanding that lies at the very heart of this process: God's love comes first. It has always existed. It was before the beginning of time and before the formation of the world. It was before the creation of human beings and before the onset of human sin. This love is, as St. Paul says, the very ground of our being, the most fundamental reality.

God acted first. God took the initiative and created us, out of love. God did not simply respond in love to our sin. This means that we were created for a reason, that we have a purpose for our life, and this purpose is given to us by God. Our very existence is a gift from God. This is why we are grateful; we are starting with God's love, and responding to it, rather than looking at our own failings.

Health professionals know that attitude plays a large role in the success of any exercise program. If we start exercising because we feel we have no choice, we resent doing it, and we are convinced we won't enjoy it, we are more likely to give up. But if we start with the attitude that we are thankful that we have bodies and that we are able to exercise at all, that these are blessings, then there is a greater chance we will stick with it.

Spiritual exercises work the same way. We start by being thankful that we exist and that we have bodies, minds, and wills that we can use. These are not just givens that we can take for granted; they are blessings. Recognizing this is much more effective than focusing on our needs and our faults. We know that we have made mistakes in the past and that we will continue to make mistakes. We are imperfect. But nothing can take these gifts away from us. So it is appropriate to be grateful to the Giver: God.

Interestingly, recent medical research has shown that patients recovering from surgery — and in fact anyone who is ill or injured — heals much more quickly with an attitude of hope and gratitude than one of depression or despair. Popular writer Dr. Bernie Siegel has written several books detailing his work with cancer patients using this approach. He tells story after story about people who chose to be positive — adopted it as their basic mind-set despite their suffering — and then experienced surprising recoveries. In another area, many parenting experts approach discipline problems by first focusing on a child's positive qualities and appreciating them.

In other words, the parent must be thankful for the child before trying to correct the child. Marriage counselors give similar advice to couples. List your spouse's good points first, they say, before broaching any complaints. Keep them in the front of your mind and be thankful for them; this forms a foundation necessary for solving difficulties.

Gratitude, then, is important not only for the times we formally pray and worship. It touches, and is essential to, all aspects of our lives, because all these aspects are connected. Physical, spiritual, mental, emotional: God works through all parts of us and all these parts reflect God. We have good reason to be grateful!

As Christians, we are most grateful for the sacrifice of Jesus Christ — his dying for our sins so we might be saved and reconciled with God. This mystery is what we celebrate in the Mass with the Eucharist. In the original Greek, the word "Eucharist" means "thanksgiving." Receiving the body and blood of Christ in the form of bread and wine is our way of giving thanks to God for the gift of his Son.

Being grateful to God does not always come easily, however. Many of us have a hard time seeing God as the generous giver of gifts, the one who loves us without reservation. Perhaps because of our childhood relationship with our parents or because of some trauma, we may see God as a harsh, unforgiving figure, or a cold and distant one. We may feel that we have to earn God's approval by good behavior. We may believe that God will never really love us.

Such images of God, growing out of our past, are deeply embedded and can have a strong effect on us, even as adults. But we need to try to step back a bit, to look at ourselves and our negative emotions and reactions with some detachment. We can try to understand where they come from. We can accept them and acknowledge their influence on us, and then we can ask God to help us move beyond them. We can ask for the grace to realize that God is much more than anything we can construct or imagine, much greater than any image or doctrine.

VII. Exercise: Gratitude
   (10 minutes alone; 10 minutes in pairs; 10 minutes in the whole group)

1. Say something like:

   > *At the beginning of this session, we saw and heard in the presentation some of the things for which we can be grateful. Now, please spend a few minutes in silence, thinking about how you would answer the questions, "What am I most grateful for? Why?" You can jot down your response briefly in your Participant's Book, on page 34.*

   After everyone has done this (about ten minutes), ask people if they noticed anything about how they chose their answer. What did they think about? What did they focus on? (For example, someone might realize, "First, I thought about my job, because I do like it. But then I focused on more basic things, like cooking and gardening, which I really do enjoy.") Have them make a note of this, too.

2. Divide the group into pairs. Explain that people will be sharing their responses to the questions with their partners. Before they start, have the pairs go to quiet places around the room (or in other rooms) so they can talk in privacy.

3. After ten minutes, call everyone back together. Have each person tell the whole group what his or her partner said. Take about ten minutes for this discussion.

4. Pay attention to what people say. Are there any patterns to the responses? Ask the group if anyone notices a pattern. If so, what is it?

VIII. Looking Ahead to Session Two (5 minutes)

1. Tell the group that there are four things for them to do before the next meeting. First, tell them about a comment Ignatius once made, that every sin, at its heart, is a sin of ingratitude. Ask people to reflect on this over the next week. What might Ignatius have meant by this? Do people agree? Why or why not?

2. Another assignment is to read the Acts of the Apostles, chapter 10, verses 1–23. Explain that the group will be sharing their thoughts about this passage at the beginning of the next session.

   Give people a brief description of what happens in the passage and the things they should be looking for as they read.

   In this passage, two people have visions: Peter and Cornelius. They are both rather shaken by their experience and don't know what to make of it. Through these visions, the stage is set for the two men to meet each other. God tells Cornelius to send for Peter and then tells Peter to go to Cornelius when he is summoned. It's all at God's initiative. Pay attention in this reading to how Peter and Cornelius are described. How are they different? How are they alike? How does Peter see himself?

3. Ask people to try the Examen at home a few times over the next week. To help them with this, ask them to read the article on the Examen by Dennis Hamm, beginning on page 25 of the Participant's Book. It also is found on page 36 in this book.

4. Finally, ask people to read the sections on sin and being attentive (Participant's Book, pages 38–44) before the next session.

IX. Closing Prayer (5 minutes)

Lead the group in a short spontaneous prayer. Invite anyone who wishes to offer specific prayers to do so.

Note: The following is background material for you, for the discussion of this passage of Acts, which you will lead next week. Use it as you see fit.

ACTS 10:1–23: PARADIGM SHIFTS

Many of us can remember — or if we can't, we've heard about — the 1950s as a time when we Catholics learned our religion from manuals. It seemed that all truth had been codified, Catholicism was set, and the script was determined. All we had to do was learn our role and play it as well as possible.

But the Second Vatican Council began to change the script. Some of the conventions, and many other things, began to be questioned. The role of the laity was questioned. The way the Church was defined was questioned. The way missionary work was done was questioned. The way Scripture was understood and used was questioned.

All of this has been disturbing for some people and liberating for others. To understand it, people use a concept from science called a "paradigm shift." This was originally a scientific term that described the jump in understanding from Ptolemy's concept of the universe to that of Copernicus. The Ptolemaic understanding saw an earth fixed in space, around which all the other heavenly bodies revolved. It was a commonsense view of the universe, because to our senses it does appear that the sun rises and sets and that the earth is standing still. Copernicus, on the other hand, postulated that the sun is fixed and that the planets, including the earth, revolve around the sun. We have become so used to this latter way of understanding the universe that we don't appreciate how troubling it was for the people of the sixteenth century. It required a major shift in their thinking. In particular, it was very troubling for theologians to consider the possibility that the earth might not be the center of God's creation.

We have experienced other such paradigm shifts in the last several hundred years, such as the change in physics from Newton's theory to Einstein's, and in medicine from pre–germ theory to post–germ theory. Some paradigm shifts are massive, causing changes far and wide. One such shift was when the early church came to understand that Jesus was both fully human and fully divine. Other shifts are more recent, such as the changes in our understanding of church, mission, ministry, and the intersection of culture, economics, and religion that took place after the Second Vatican Council.

A very important part of growing as human beings, and growing in holiness, is experiencing and accepting changes in perspective. We all resist change, especially any change in religious perspective. Such change can be frightening. It tends to disrupt our routines and challenge our certitudes. It makes us wonder if everything we have believed before is false — or perhaps the proposed change is false.

Why is a change in perspective so essential and yet so difficult? It is essential because it grows out of intelligence, and intelligence is one of the most precious gifts we receive from God. And it is difficult because this same intelligence of ours is very complex. On the one hand, it wants us to expand and grow and deepen in understanding. On the other hand, it also wants to create a safe haven for us, to provide us with sure guidelines, to make it possible for us to control our destinies and plan our lives. But God and reality keep reminding us that our knowing is limited and that our understanding comes in increments — hence our need to experience those pesky paradigm shifts. This concept is also linked to the idea of theology rightly thought of as faith seeking understanding.

St. Peter has a conversion, a paradigm shift. It starts in Acts 10. As a result of his discipleship under Jesus, Peter has become a Jew of strict observance. He is determined to observe all of the Mosaic laws, as the Jews of his day understood them. He is determined to observe the dietary laws and the laws forbidding Jews to consort with Gentiles. On top of that, he feels he has to set a good example for the community of disciples, who have also become observant Jews and who consider him the leader.

But God has other plans. God initiates an incredible change, not by acting on Peter, but by acting on a Gentile — and not just a Gentile but a Roman, a military man, a centurion. If there were any person the Jews would want to keep at a distance, it would be someone like Cornelius. But God will not be deterred by our human prejudices and fears and customs, not even the religious ones.

In Caesarea there was a man named Cornelius, a centurion of the Italian Cohort, as it was called. He was a devout man who feared God with all his household; he gave alms generously to the people and prayed constantly to God. One afternoon at about three o'clock he had a vision in which he clearly saw an angel of God coming in and saying to him, "Cornelius." He stared at him in terror and said, "What is it, Lord?" He answered, "Your prayers and your alms have ascended as a memorial before God. Now send men to Joppa for a certain Simon who is called Peter; he is lodging with Simon, a tanner, whose house is by the seaside." When the angel who spoke to him had left, he called two of his slaves and a devout soldier from the ranks of those who served him, and after telling them everything, he sent them to Joppa.

God has clearly taken the initiative here. He has touched Cornelius. But what will Peter do when he is confronted with an invitation from a person the Law tells him is forbidden, off-limits, unclean? But God touches Peter as well.

About noon the next day, as they were on their journey and approaching the city, Peter went up on the roof to pray. He became hungry and wanted something to eat; and while it was being prepared, he fell into a trance. He saw the heaven opened and something like a large sheet coming down, being lowered to the ground by its four corners. In it were all kinds of four-footed creatures and reptiles and birds of the air. Then he heard a voice saying, "Get up, Peter; kill and eat." But Peter said, "By no means, Lord; for I have never eaten anything that is profane or unclean." The voice said to him again, a second time, "What God has made clean, you must not call profane." This happened three times, and the thing was suddenly taken up to heaven.

So Peter thinks he just got a lesson about food, and he thinks the insight he has been given is that no food is to be considered unclean. But in a few minutes, Peter is going to realize that this vision is not about food at all.

Now while Peter was greatly puzzled about what to make of the vision that he had seen, suddenly the men sent by Cornelius appeared. They were asking for Simon's house and were standing by the gate. They called out to ask whether Simon, who was called Peter, was staying there. While Peter was still thinking about the vision, the Spirit said to him, "Look, three men are searching for you. Now get up, go down, and go with them without hesitation; for I have sent them." So Peter went down to the men and said, "I am the one you are looking for; what is the reason for your coming?" They answered, "Cornelius, a centurion, an upright and God-fearing man, who is well spoken of by the whole Jewish nation, was directed by a holy angel to send for you to come to his house and to hear what you have to say." So Peter invited them in and gave them lodging.

Notice that Peter's instincts are quite good. He does not receive the delegates from Cornelius reluctantly. Rather, he invites them in and shows them hospitality — which is itself an unusual thing for him, a devout Jew, to do. Although Peter does not know it, this marks the beginning of a major shift in his perspective.

RUMMAGING FOR GOD:
Praying Backward through Your Day
by Dennis Hamm, S.J.

About twenty years ago, at breakfast and during the few hours that followed, I had a small revelation. This happened while

I was living in a small community of five Jesuits, all gradu-
ate students in New Haven, Connecticut. I was alone in the
kitchen with my cereal and the *New York Times,* when another
Jesuit came in and said: "I had the weirdest dream just before
I woke up. It was a liturgical dream. The lector had just read
the first reading and proceeded to announce, 'The responsorial refrain today is, *If at first you don't succeed, try, try
again.'* Whereupon the entire congregation soberly repeated,
'If at first you don't succeed, try, try again.'" We both thought
this enormously funny. At first, I wasn't sure just *why* this was
so humorous. After all, almost everyone would assent to the
courageous truth of the maxim, "If at first..." It has to be a
cross-cultural truism ("Keep on truckin'"). Why, then, would
these words sound so incongruous in a liturgy?

A little later in the day, I stumbled onto a clue. Another, similar phrase popped into my mind: "If today you hear his voice,
harden not your hearts" (Ps. 95). It struck me that that sen-
tence has exactly the same rhythm and the same syntax as:
"If at first you don't succeed, try, try again." Both begin with an
"if" clause and end in an imperative. Both have seven beats.
Maybe that was one of the unconscious sources of the humor.

The try-try-again statement sounds like the harden-not-
your-heart refrain, yet what a contrast! The latter is clearly
biblical, a paraphrase of a verse from a psalm, one frequently
used as a responsorial refrain at the Eucharist. The former,
you know instinctively, is probably not in the Bible, not even
in Proverbs. It is true enough, as far as it goes, but it does not
go far enough. There is nothing of faith in it, no sense of God.
The sentiment of the line from Psalm 95, however, expresses
a conviction central to Hebrew and Christian faith, that we
live a life in dialogue with God. The contrast between those
two seven-beat lines has, ever since, been for me a paradigm
illustrating that truth.

Yet how do we hear the voice of God? Our Christian tradition has at least four answers to that question. First, along with the faithful of most religions, we perceive the divine in what God has made, creation itself (that insight sits at the heart of Christian moral thinking). Second, we hear God's voice in the Scriptures, which we even call "the word of God." Third, we hear God in the authoritative teaching of the Church, the living tradition of our believing community. Finally, we hear God by attending to our experience, and interpreting it in the light of all those other ways of hearing the divine voice — the structures of creation, the Bible, the living tradition of the community.

The phrase, "If *today* you hear his voice," implies that the divine voice must somehow be accessible in our daily experience, for we are creatures who live one day at a time. If God wants to communicate with us, it has to happen in the course of a twenty-four-hour day, for we live in no other time. And how do we go about this kind of listening? Long tradition has provided a helpful tool, which we call the examination of consciousness today. "Rummaging for God" is an expression that suggests going through a drawer full of stuff, feeling around, looking for something that you are sure must be in there somewhere. I think that image catches some of the feel of what is classically known in church language as the prayer of "Examen."

The Examen, or examination, of conscience is an ancient practice in the Church. In fact, even before Christianity, the Pythagoreans and the Stoics promoted a version of the practice. It is what most of us Catholics were taught to do to prepare for confession. In that form, the Examen was a matter of examining one's life in terms of the Ten Commandments to see how daily behavior stacked up against those divine criteria. St. Ignatius includes it as one of the exercises in his manual *The Spiritual Exercises.*

It is still a salutary thing to do but wears thin as a lifelong, daily practice. It is hard to motivate yourself to keep searching your experience for how you sinned. In recent decades, spiritual writers have worked with the implication that *conscience* in Romance languages like French (*conscience*) and Spanish (*conciencia*) means more than our English word "conscience," in the sense of moral awareness and judgment; it also means "consciousness."

Now prayer that deals with the full contents of your *consciousness* lets you cast your net much more broadly than prayer that limits itself to the contents of conscience, or moral awareness. A number of people — most famously, George Aschenbrenner, S.J., in an article in *Review for Religious* (1971) — have developed this idea in profoundly practical ways. Recently, the Institute of Jesuit Sources in St. Louis published a fascinating reflection by Joseph Tetlow, S.J., called *The Most Postmodern Prayer: American Jesuit Identity and the Examen of Conscience, 1920–1990.*

What I am proposing here is a way of doing the Examen that works for me. It puts a special emphasis on feelings, for reasons that I hope will become apparent. First, I describe the format. Second, I invite you to spend a few minutes actually doing it. Third, I describe some of the consequences that I have discovered to flow from this kind of prayer.

A Five-Step Method

1. *Pray for light.* Since we are not simply daydreaming or reminiscing but rather looking for some sense of how the Spirit of God is leading us, it only makes sense to pray for some illumination. The goal is not simply memory but graced understanding. That's a gift from God

devoutly to be begged. "Lord, help me understand this blooming, buzzing confusion."

2. *Review the day in thanksgiving.* Note how different this is from looking immediately for your sins. Nobody likes to poke around in the memory bank to uncover smallness, weakness, lack of generosity. But everybody likes to fondle beautiful gifts, and that is precisely what the past twenty-four hours contain — gifts of existence, work, relationships, food, challenges. Gratitude is the foundation of our whole relationship with God. So use whatever cues help you to walk through the day from the moment of awakening — even the dreams you recall upon awakening. Walk through the past twenty-four hours, from hour to hour, from place to place, task to task, person to person, thanking the Lord for every gift you encounter.

3. *Review the feelings that surface in the play of the day.* Our feelings, positive and negative, the painful and the pleasing, are clear signals of where the action was during the day. Simply pay attention to any and all of those feelings as they surface, the whole range: delight, boredom, fear, anticipation, resentment, anger, peace, contentment, impatience, desire, hope, regret, shame, uncertainty, compassion, disgust, gratitude, pride, rage, doubt, confidence, admiration, shyness — whatever was there. Some of us may be hesitant to focus on feelings in this over-psychologized age, but I believe that these feelings are the liveliest index to what is happening in our lives. This leads us to the fourth moment.

4. *Choose one of those feelings (positive or negative) and pray from it.* That is, choose the remembered feeling that most caught your attention. The feeling is a sign that

something important was going on. Now simply express spontaneously the prayer that surfaces as you attend to the source of the feeling — praise, petition, contrition, cry for help or healing, whatever.

5. *Look toward tomorrow.* Using your appointment calendar if that helps, face your immediate future. What feelings surface as you look at the tasks, meetings, and appointments that face you? Fear? Delight? Anticipation? Self-doubt? Temptation to procrastinate? Zestful planning? Regret? Weakness? Whatever it is, turn it into prayer — for help, for healing, whatever comes spontaneously. To conclude the Examen, say the Lord's Prayer.

A mnemonic for recalling the five points: LT3Fs (light, thanks, feelings, focus, future). *Try it!* Take a few minutes to pray through the past twenty-four hours, and toward the next twenty-four hours, with that five-point format.

Consequences

Here are some of the consequences flowing from this kind of prayer:

1. There is always something to pray about. For a person who does this kind of prayer at least once a day, there is never the question: What should I talk to God about? Until you die, you always have a past twenty-four hours, and you always have some feelings about what's next.

2. The gratitude moment is worthwhile in itself. "Dedicate yourselves to gratitude," Paul tells the Colossians. Even if we drift off into slumber after reviewing the gifts of the day, we have praised the Lord.

3. We learn to face the Lord where we are, as we are. There is no other way to be present to God, of course, but we often fool ourselves into thinking that we have to "put on our best face" before we address our God.

4. We learn to respect our feelings. Feelings count. They are morally neutral until we make some choice about acting upon or dealing with them. But if we don't attend to them, we miss what they have to tell us about the quality of our lives.

5. Praying from feelings, we are liberated from them. An unattended emotion can dominate and manipulate us. Attending to and praying from and about the persons and situations that give rise to the emotions helps us to cease being unwitting slaves of our emotions.

6. We actually find something to bring to confession. That is, we stumble across our sins without making them the primary focus.

7. We can experience an inner healing. People have found that praying about (as opposed to fretting about or denying) feelings leads to a healing of mental life. We probably get a head start on our dreamwork when we do this.

8. This kind of prayer helps us get over our Deism. Deism is belief in a sort of "clockmaker" God, a God who does indeed exist but does not have much, if anything, to do with his people's ongoing life. The God we have come to know through our Jewish and Christian experience is more present than we usually think.

9. Praying this way is an antidote to the spiritual dis-ease of Pelagianism. Pelagianism was the heresy that approached life with God as a do-it-yourself project ("If

at first you don't succeed . . ."), whereas a true theology of grace and freedom sees life as response to God's love ("If today you hear God's voice . . .").

A final thought. How can anyone dare to say that paying attention to felt experience is a listening to the voice of God? On the face of it, it does sound like a dangerous presumption. But, notice, I am not equating memory with the voice of God. I am saying that, if we are to listen for the God who creates and sustains us, we need to take seriously and prayerfully the meeting between the creatures we are and all else that God holds lovingly in existence. That "interface" is the felt experience of my day. It deserves prayerful attention. It is a big part of how we know and respond to God.

Being Attentive

I. Welcome and Opening Prayer (10 minutes)

II. Processing Scripture (25 minutes)

1. Begin by asking people, in general, how they did over the past week with their reading and other assignments. Did anyone have difficulty? Does anyone have any comments or feedback? In particular, ask about people's experience with the Examen. How did it go? How do they feel about it? Explain that it's important to persist with it, that they need to be regular in doing it. Over time, if they are faithful to it, they will notice that a pattern will develop. Finally, stress the importance of practicing gratitude.

2. Have the Scripture passage that was assigned last time (Acts 10:1–23) read out loud. Ask members of the group to take turns.

3. Afterward, ask for people's reflections on the passage. Briefly note the comments on newsprint.

III. Presentation: Horizons (10 minutes)

1. Transition: Talk about, if it hasn't come up in the discussion already, how Peter has a certain way of seeing himself and the world. He is a devout follower of Jewish laws, and that colors his perspective. Some foods

are clean; others are unclean. Some people are acceptable; others are not. There is no middle ground. Then the
vision comes, and Peter starts to change his thinking.

2. Make the comment that we all have particular ways of
   seeing the world — just like Peter. His religious beliefs
   shaped how he saw things. Our religious beliefs and
   our culture affect our perceptions as well. We believe
   that some things are valuable, some are not; some are
   good and some are evil. And this colors how we see
   them or even *if* we see them. For example, if we have
   decided that something is not important, we may not
   see it because we don't focus on it. It is simply not true
   that everyone looking at the same situation will see the
   same thing. Talk about how eyewitnesses to an event
   all see it slightly differently (sometimes to the point of
   relating totally contradictory accounts). Our individual
   talents and inclinations also affect our perceptions. If, for
   instance, we like art and know a lot about it, we will see
   a painting or a sculpture very differently from a person
   who has no interest in or knowledge of art. If basketball
   is our favorite sport, we will not see the same basketball game as someone who knows nothing about it. This
   holds true for music, literature, gardening, cars — all the
   elements of our world.

3. We see the world in a particular way because this is how
   we make sense of the world. From the time we are born,
   we have to figure out everything around us. We have
   to assign meaning to everything; we couldn't function
   otherwise, if we were bombarded by constant stimuli, all
   equally important. It's somewhat of a filtering process,
   and it is essential to our growth as human beings.

4. How we see the world is based largely on what we have learned from other people as we grow up (our parents, friends, neighbors, teachers) and other outside sources (books, movies, newspapers, etc.). So our view of the world is based on belief, and our belief has been shaped heavily by other people and other influences.

5. We have each constructed our own view of the world out of these beliefs, experiences, ideas, and perceptions. For each one of us, "my world" is the sum total of what I know, experience, care about, and am interested in. It is not the world in its entirety; it can't be, because no one person can experience everything. It's the world as I know it and live in it. And, within each person's world, some elements are central — extremely important — and others are peripheral. We don't feel the same about everything.

6. "My world" can contain mistakes. We may have an inaccurate perception of something, because everyone around us also has this perception and we simply adopted it. We may believe something that is untrue, because an experience led us to make a decision based on incomplete information. For a variety of reasons, we all tend to have some mistakes in our world — and some of these mistakes may be very important parts of our world.

7. People's worlds can overlap. A teacher and a welder can hold similar views on social policy. A farmer and an artist can share a passion for ecology. This overlapping makes possible friendship, community, and cooperation. But sometimes people's worlds never overlap. This may be because their central or dominant elements are diametrically opposed, such as a pacifist and a hawk or

a fervent religious believer and an atheist. It may also be because these people's entire worlds are so very different, as sometimes happens with members of different cultures.

8. "My" world changes over time. There is a constant, active exchange between our own minds and wills and the information we receive from others. This interaction is a lifelong process. If I learn more, my world becomes larger. If I eliminate mistaken views or ideas, it becomes less distorted.

9. Over time, I want "my" world to grow and change to coincide more and more with the way the world really is. Only God sees the whole world the way it actually is—and only God loves it for what it is.

In order for my world to grow and change, I need first to be attentive to it. I must step back from it and watch it, pay attention to it. What does it look like? What's important in it? What's not in it at all? We need to pay special attention to what's not in our world, to our boundaries and limits. These are our horizons. Especially as church leaders, we must be aware of our horizons and our world, as the first step to trying to make it more like *the* world—God's world. And part of this is becoming aware of the mistakes in our world, the things that are not accurate, not valid, not true. Becoming aware of them is the first step to eliminating them.

As we pay attention to the world we've constructed, we are attentive to the gifts God has given us, and we are grateful. We also begin to notice the occasions when we misuse these gifts. This awareness is connected to the first week of Ignatius's Spiritual Exercises. Ignatius put it this way: Ask God for the grace to know sin in your life.

Note: Tell people not to be put off by the word "sin." If you wish, discuss the article in the Participant's Book (pages 38–40), which they have read for this session.

IV. Exercise: My Horizons
(15 minutes alone, 15 minutes in pairs,
20 minutes in the whole group)

1. Give each person a large sheet of paper or newsprint and colored markers. Tell people to draw their horizons. They draw themselves at the center, and then ask themselves the question: "As a church leader, what am I paying attention to on a regular basis? Where are my time and energy going?" They can include: the people they work with; their duties; their beliefs; their ideas, hopes, and fears; their projects and plans; their possessions; their memories. They should have at least twelve such elements.

   Tell them to put all these elements in their horizons. Those that are closer to the center are the ones that are more important to them as church leaders. Those that are farther out are less important. They should flag anything that is either life-giving or discouraging. Is anything missing? Is anything not being used enough? Are there any simmering problems? What are the opportunities and what are the obstacles?

2. When people are finished, have them pair off and share their horizons with their partners. Then bring everyone back to the whole group and ask them for their insights. What did they notice about their horizons? Can they see any patterns? Are they surprised about where the elements of their lives fit in? Do they see anything they want to change?

Example: Horizons of a Laywoman

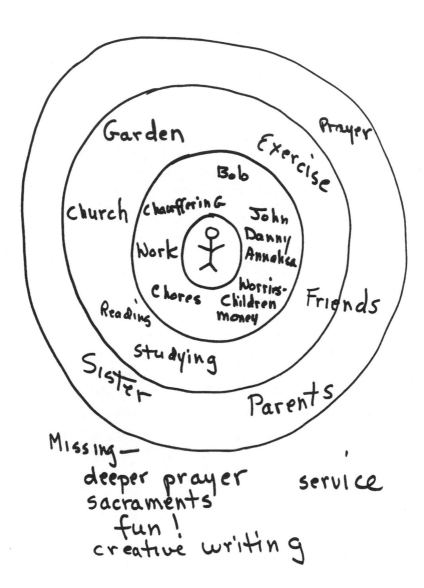

V. Looking Ahead to Session Three (10 minutes)

1. Talk about the assignments for the next session. The first is to keep reading the Acts of the Apostles: chapter 10, verses 23 to 35. Briefly talk about the passage, explaining that this is where Peter and Cornelius meet. Note how unusual it is for a devout Jew to associate with a Gentile. Tell people to be aware of the two uses of words having to do with sight. What do they think is going on in the passage? What is happening to Peter?

2. Another assignment is to practice being attentive. Read aloud the instructions in the Participant's Book, page 49.

   Choose one day during the next week and try to be attentive to your experience throughout that day. What happens around you, with the people in your community? What happens within you? How do you react to what happens? Where do your time and energy go? What was consoling? What was problematic? Are you pleased with what you see? Do you see any patterns? What are they?

   Ask people to write down their thoughts on this exercise.

3. Finally, ask the group members to read 'A Lesson in Semantics," "The Dynamism of Consciousness," and "A Personal Narrative" on pages 51–55 in the Participant's Book before the next session.

VI. Closing Prayer (5 minutes)

Offer a spontaneous prayer or ask a member of the group to do it.

Note: The following is background material for the discussion next week on Acts 10:23–35, which you will lead. Use it as you see fit.

ACTS 10:23–35: PETER AND CORNELIUS

The next day he got up and went with them, and some of the believers from Joppa accompanied him. The following day they came to Caesarea. Cornelius was expecting them and had called together his relatives and close friends. On Peter's arrival Cornelius met him, and falling at his feet, worshiped him. But Peter made him get up, saying, "Stand up; I am only a mortal." And as he talked with him, he went in and found that many had assembled; and he said to them, "You yourselves know that it is unlawful for a Jew to associate with or to visit a Gentile; but God has shown me that I should not call anyone profane or unclean. So when I was sent for, I came without objection. Now may I ask why you sent for me?"

Cornelius replied, "Four days ago at this very hour, at three o'clock, I was praying in my house when suddenly a man in dazzling clothes stood before me. He said, 'Cornelius, your prayer has been heard and your alms have been remembered before God. Send therefore to Joppa and ask for Simon, who is called Peter; he is staying in the home of Simon, a tanner, by the sea.' Therefore I sent for you immediately, and you have been kind enough to come. So now all of us are here in the presence of God to listen to all that the Lord has commanded you to say."

Then Peter began to speak to them: "I truly understand that God shows no partiality, but in every nation anyone who fears him and does what is right is acceptable to him."

This is the paradigm shift. This is what challenges all the rules that are in Peter's head about dealing with Gentiles. This is the beginning of his conversion. Can you see what a huge shift of perspective this is for Peter? Did you sense any resistance in him? What do you think his companions in Jerusalem will think when he goes back and tells them that he entered the house of a Gentile?

There is yet more to come. But for the present, try to think whether you have experienced any shifts in your religious understanding: about the Church, about God, about the Eucharist, about devotions, about how you see non-Catholics, about how you understand the parish church, about how you understand prayer. Also think about whether you've experienced resistance in changing your perspective. Peter's story can help us reflect on our own story. It can help us realize that change will happen, that we should not be distressed at our own resistance, and that very often it is God who challenges us and often through the most unlikely people.

Exploring (Being Intelligent)

I. Welcome and Opening Prayer (10 minutes)

II. Processing the Assignments and Scripture (20 minutes)

1. Ask for people's feedback on the exercise to be attentive for a day. What did they notice about where they put their time and energy? What did they find to be consoling? What was difficult? What part did other people — their communities — play? Did they see any patterns? As people talk, write their comments on the newsprint.

2. Have different members of the group read out loud the Scripture passage that was assigned (Acts 10:23–35). Ask people what they think of the passage. What were their reactions to it? Write their comments on newsprint.

III. Presentation: Exploring and the Dynamism of Consciousness (20 minutes)

1. Make a transition by pointing out a change in Peter's understanding of a very important element in his world: what is clean and unclean, what to include in his life and what to exclude. This change occurred because Peter,

presented with new information, new input, started asking questions about things. He wondered what was happening. He didn't dismiss the new data just because it conflicted with his previous understanding.

2. Explain that the word "exploring" is used here more as a verb than a noun. It involves looking closely at things, puzzling about them and examining them. It requires being open to new information and new data. It means we are constantly making corrections to our understanding. In short, it's discovery, trying to understand our world by exploring it. It requires effort.

3. This exploration, this effort to understand that we saw Peter make is basic to human beings. It is the second element in a four-part process: the dynamism of consciousness.

4. This dynamism is how we work. It is the human operational structure of our consciousness. To borrow from the world of technology, the dynamism is something like our operating system, much like a computer's operating system (which lies under what we see on the screen) is for a computer. It's the foundation. It underlies all the particular things we think and we do. It is how we know what we know and how we make our decisions. And, like a computer's operating system, it's running all the time in the background, largely unnoticed by us — but utterly crucial. What we are doing here is bringing this dynamism into the foreground to get a good look at it.

5. However, don't be misled by the computer analogy. This dynamism is given to us by God and is not machine-like at all. It is our inner drive toward truth and value. It is not a recipe or a formula, a technique where you

follow the correct steps in the correct order and always arrive at the desired outcome. Rather, it is a very human, organic process, where, if we are attentive and faithful to it, we are moved along through these four operations or phases by the restlessness, the hunger and thirst, that lies at our very core. For this reason, this dynamism is often felt as questions that keep pushing us along.

6. What this dynamism is *not* is esoteric, trendy, or mystical. It's not a New Age phenomenon. Learning about it does not require total self-absorption. Finally, it is not spectacular or extraordinary (usually) or something experienced only by a privileged few, such as saints. It is ordinary, commonplace, natural. When you pay attention to what's happening within you when you're trying to understand a situation or make a decision — this is the dynamism at work.

7. Give an overview of the four elements — what we might call the four capacities — of this dynamism of consciousness. Begin with a simple story, from your own experience, that shows the four capacities at work. (Below is a sample to get you thinking.) Then, as you outline the elements, go back to the story and point out where you can see them at work.

> I walked out' to the parking lot of the mall, my arms laden with shopping bags and packages. I was pretty sure I remembered where I had parked my red Voyager minivan, about three rows to the left of the exit door of the mall. I saw it, only five cars up in the third row, and hurried over. I shifted the packages, dug my keys out of my pocket, and put the car key into the lock. It went in — but it

wouldn't turn. I frowned. Why was the key not working? Had one of the children been playing with it
and bent it? Had I done something to it? I tried
again, and again it wouldn't move. I sighed and put
my bags and boxes on the ground. I held the key
up close to my face and looked at it carefully. Was
it the right key? It was. Was it twisted? No. Were
any of the notches chipped? No. A new, frightening thought hit me: had someone tried to steal the
car and damaged the lock? I looked at the door
and didn't see any scratches on it. Then, out of
the corner of my eye, I noticed something. There
was a blue and gold tassel hanging from the inside
front mirror, with plastic letters that said 99. It was
a graduation tassel — only none of my children had
graduated from school yet. I walked around to the
back of the car and noticed something else: a bright
yellow sticker on the bumper that read, "Troop-
ers are the best protection." I didn't have such a
bumper sticker. What was going on? Then I looked
down at the license plate and read, NKC 789. That
wasn't my license plate number. Oh — maybe this
wasn't my car. I peered into the window and saw
black upholstery and a pile of CDs on the floor. My
idea was confirmed; this wasn't my car. I looked
around me and, four cars further up, saw another
red Voyager van. This one had my license plate on
it. Feeling sheepish, I picked up my packages and
walked over to it.

8. The first capacity is **being attentive.** We have already
talked about this in Session Two. This happens at the
level of experience — when we use our senses, when we

imagine things, when we notice things. It's when we pay attention to what is going on around us and within us. It means, as we did in the exercise last week, trying to step back and notice our noticing. The question felt here is: What am I experiencing?

9. The second capacity is **exploring.** Lonergan called this being intelligent. We gather data. We look for clues, ideas, connections; we form hypotheses. We are trying to make sense of what we're experiencing, trying to find a pattern that explains it and gives it meaning. We have a sense of wonder about things, which, in the form of questions, is what takes us from being attentive to being explorative. The questions we ask are: What's going on here? How can I make sense of it?

10. The third capacity is **discerning.** This is the level of judgment. We're trying to discern what is real and true, based on the questions we've asked and the evidence we've collected. We are testing our understanding. We are coming up with possible explanations. The questions we ask are: Do my hypotheses fit the data? Is my explanation correct? Does my understanding correspond to what is true?

11. The fourth capacity is **being responsible.** This is the level of decision. Now that we have gathered data, come to an understanding of them, and made a judgment about what is true — we act. We take a stand; we make choices. We use what we have learned from the three previous elements to decide what is real, what is true, what is valuable, and we base our action on this judgment. The question we ask here is: What should I do?

12. These capacities are always at work within us. We never really stop using them. They don't form a straight line on which we move from beginning to end and then we're done. They actually form more of a spiral. We keep looping back over all the capacities. When we make a decision (capacity four) and take action, we change the situation. This means we have new input, new data, to experience (capacity one), to try to understand (capacity two) and make judgments about (capacity three). The process keeps repeating, and this is how we grow in knowledge over time.

13. When it operates the way it's supposed to, it's a self-correcting process. If we make an incorrect decision, then we go back and ask what went wrong. Was our judgment invalid? Was our data insufficient? Did we ask the right questions? It's important to pay attention to the whole process, because making good decisions requires using all four of these capacities well. Skipping any one of them, or doing one incompletely, will hinder the process — for example, if we don't pay attention to our experience, or don't ask any questions about it, or don't take the time to make an informed judgment.

14. *Note:* The concept that follows — of personal authenticity — is key. This is a brief introduction to it. Tell participants that you will be revisiting it in later sessions.

PERSONAL AUTHENTICITY

God gave us these capacities. They're basic to who we are; they are not a system somebody invented. They are how we naturally function when we're operating the way God wants us to.

When we are attentive to and responsive to this dynamism within us, we are being true to our best self — not just true to our self, because our self can be distorted. The definition of **personal authenticity** is being true to our own best self. It's not a one-time effort but a lifelong process of cooperating with the fundamental, God-given dynamism of the human spirit (human consciousness).

We cannot be authentic in isolation. By its very nature, authenticity is a communal endeavor, involving other people. For example, we have to let others point out to us things we haven't noticed, because any one person's experience is incomplete. We have to consider the questions that other people raise, because no one person can think of all the possible questions in a situation. When we do the same thing for other people, we in turn are helping them in their efforts to be authentic.

This sounds like hard work, and it is. But leadership depends on authenticity — both our own personal authenticity and our efforts to help others be authentic. Yet we do have a valuable tool to help us with this endeavor. This tool is the Examen, which we have introduced to you. We will learn that over time, doing the Examen consistently and with faithfulness helps us build an awareness of ourselves as a dynamic person in relationship with God.

We have all heard of Archbishop Oscar Romero, the archbishop of San Salvador who was assassinated in 1980 while he was saying Mass. We know him as a martyr. He spoke out against the systematic and violent oppression of the poor — and their supporters — in the poor, class-stratified society of El Salvador, and he was killed for doing it. But fewer people know that it was a winding journey that brought Oscar Romero

to that place. He didn't start his priestly career already sup-
porting the poor peasants of his country. He began as a priest
with many privileges, who studied in Rome before his ordina-
tion, served briefly as a country priest, and then was secretary
to El Salvador's Bishops' Conference for twenty-three years.
He was an able administrator and was made a bishop in 1970.
Even after being made archbishop of San Salvador in 1977,
he did not immediately criticize the centuries-old alliance of
the wealthy landowners, the government, and the hierarchy
of the Church, the alliance that kept those groups comfortable and powerful while most of the people were poor and
suffering. It took the murder of a priest — one who had been
working to help the poor — to shock Romero into taking a
stand. We know what happened then: he used his position
and all the means he could, including the archdiocesan radio
station, to speak against the brutal oppression. He received
warnings and death threats, but he kept going. He even pre-
dicted his own violent death. But he was compelled to keep
preaching the Gospel and what it meant in his particular situation until he was stopped by force. He followed God's call
faithfully, wherever it took him — the mark of a truly authentic
person.

Authenticity does not always result in martyrdom, of course.
You may remember the story of the young boy from New Jersey who was in New York City and was struck by the large
numbers of homeless people he saw. Despite a cold wind,
most of these people were dressed in thin, ragged clothes.
They all looked hungry. When he returned to his home, the
boy told his mother about what he had seen and announced
that he wanted to help. They talked it over, and he decided
to go to New York City and bring sandwiches and blankets to
homeless people. His mother drove him. He and his family

started by undertaking this mission themselves, but soon other people heard about what he was doing and the project grew. Classmates, neighbors, and other people donated blankets and sandwiches by the carload and soon he was making trips into the city several times a week. This boy had heard the voice of God and listened attentively.

IV. Exercise: Doing the Examen (15 minutes individually, 15 minutes in pairs, 20 minutes in the whole group)

1. Tell people that they will now, individually, do the Examen. Refer them to pages 22 and 23 in the Participant's Book, which lists the steps. Tell people to take about fifteen minutes, and have them go to different corners of the room so they can have quiet.

2. After the fifteen minutes, ask people to get together with their partners and share their experiences with the Examen.

3. Then call everyone back together into the whole group. Ask for comments on and questions about the Examen. Write down comments on the newsprint. Are there any patterns?

V. Looking Ahead to Session Four (15 minutes)

1. Tell the participants to read Acts 10:36–48 and reflect on it. Ask them to think about what is happening here as Peter preaches to this group of Gentiles. How do the Jewish followers of Jesus react to what happens? How does Peter react?

2. For the second assignment, people will write their own personal narratives (refer them to page 59, no. 2 in their Participant's Book). Say something like:

   We all have stories to tell about our experiences as church leaders. Some experiences were negative; others were very positive. What I'd like you to do is identify one experience where you changed your mind about something. It could have been something very external and obvious — an obstacle, a problem, perhaps a crisis. Or it may have been something much more interior. Either way, it was something that you had to wrestle with. Then analyze the experience. Ask yourselves these questions: What happened? What was your understanding before the experience? Exactly how did your new understanding come to you? Was it progressive and logical, or sudden and intuitive? How did your understanding change? How did you feel? Try to be specific and concrete.

   Explain that they will be sharing their narratives at the next meeting. They have an example of a personal narrative in their Participant's Book, the story of John Henry Newman on page 54.

3. Ask participants to read the sections on discerning in their Participant's Book ("We Do Not Live in a Vacuum" and "A Study in Discernment," pages 63–68).

4. Finally, ask them to spend time over the next week reflecting on the meditation on the Trinity, the Annunciation, and the Nativity, which begins on page 70 of the Participant's Book. The meditation includes both the text and the drawings. They may find it fruitful to do this

several times, perhaps writing their impressions in their books (page 61).

VI. Closing Prayer

Say a short prayer to end the meeting, or ask a group member to do it.

Note: The following is background material on Acts 10:36–48 to help you lead the discussion next week. Use it as you see fit.

ACTS 10:36–48:
THE CONVERSION OF THE EARLY CHURCH

After Peter's conversion, we have the conversion of the Church itself. We have to remember that the earliest disciples of Jesus did not see themselves as anything other than faithful Jews. They thought that Jesus' intention was to reform the Judaism of their day, not to found a new religion. Even after Pentecost, they continued to see themselves as members of the synagogue. They tried to observe the dietary laws and the rules against getting too friendly with non-Jews. They certainly could have stayed just like this — still considering themselves Jews, who differed from other Jews in just one aspect. But God was not ready to let them settle back so easily into old, familiar patterns of life.

The conversion of the Church begins with Peter's decision. Listen. Peter first gives witness to the life of Jesus. Notice that he does not mention the fact that it was the Romans who crucified Jesus. He is quite delicate about this.

You know the message he sent to the people of Israel, preaching peace by Jesus Christ — he is Lord of all. That message

*spread throughout Judea, beginning in Galilee after the bap-
tism that John announced: how God anointed Jesus of Naza-
reth with the Holy Spirit and with power; how he went about
doing good and healing all who were oppressed by the devil,
for God was with him. We are witnesses to all that he did both
in Judea and in Jerusalem. They put him to death by hanging him on a tree; but God raised him on the third day and
allowed him to appear, not to all the people but to us who
were chosen by God as witnesses, and who ate and drank
with him after he rose from the dead. He commanded us to
preach to the people and to testify that he is the one ordained
by God as judge of the living and the dead. All the prophets
testify about him that everyone who believes in him receives
forgiveness of sins through his name.*

All well and good, but now God steps in and stirs things up.
He causes trouble. The unexpected happens. Peter and his
companions would never have dreamed that the Holy Spirit
would be given to these pagans. But God again refuses to be
limited by human rules.

*While Peter was still speaking, the Holy Spirit fell upon all
who heard the word. The circumcised believers who had
come with Peter were astounded that the gift of the Holy Spirit
had been poured out even on the Gentiles, for they heard them
speaking in tongues and extolling God. Then Peter said, "Can
anyone withhold the water for baptizing these people who
have received the Holy Spirit just as we have?" So he ordered
them to be baptized in the name of Jesus Christ. Then they
invited him to stay for several days.*

What is Peter doing, in ordering that the Romans be baptized? As it is, he has already been breaking rules left and
right. First, he entered the house of a pagan, which was

strictly forbidden for Jews, and then — and this is completely unthinkable — he shared their food. Now he has admitted these pagans into the community of the disciples of Jesus, a community that considers itself Jewish, without placing any requirements or conditions on them. He is not telling them that they have to become Jewish first in order to be accepted. Is this a crazy thing to do or what? Notice that the believers who had come with Peter were astonished that the Gentiles had received the Holy Spirit. Imagine how they must have felt when he ordered these pagans to be baptized!

Session Four

Discerning

I. Welcome and Opening Prayer (10 minutes)

II. Processing Assignments and Scripture (20 minutes)

1. Discuss the assignment where people were asked to analyze an instance when they changed their minds about something. What is group members' feedback on the assignment? Was it easy or difficult? Why? What kinds of things led to people's changing their minds? What happened afterward? Are there any patterns in people's experiences? Write comments on newsprint.

2. Ask one person to read the assigned Scripture passage: Acts 10:36–48. Talk about the passage. What is happening here? What might be going on in the minds of the Gentiles? What about the Jewish believers in Jesus? Again, write down what people say on the newsprint.

III. Presentation: Discerning and Progress/Decline/Redemption (20 minutes)

1. Transition by explaining that Peter, in the passage just discussed, discerns something: he discerns that baptism is for everyone who has received the Holy Spirit,

whether Jew or Gentile. This is a significant departure from Peter's customary way of thinking. Remember, he has been a devout Jew his whole life. He is committed to following the Jewish law. Jesus, to him, was the Messiah expected by the Jews, who came to Jews. But now he is changing his mind because he has discerned that Jesus is inviting non-Jews to follow him as well. How does he know this? He sees the descent of the Holy Spirit upon the Gentiles to whom he is speaking (Acts 10:44–46). This is the evidence upon which he bases his discernment.

2. Discerning is the third human capacity, the third part of the dynamism of consciousness that we have been exploring. Bernard Lonergan sometimes called this capacity being "reasonable." By this, he meant that we should have sufficient reasons for the judgments that we make. In other words, we have collected adequate evidence to determine if our idea, our hypothesis, is true or not. We have not jumped to conclusions. This describes pretty well the process Peter goes through in the reading we discussed today.

3. Notice that discerning is not the same as making a decision. Discerning is making a judgment; making a decision is making a choice and taking action based on that choice. Discerning is what you do *before* you act.

4. How do we learn to discern? What can help us in our discerning? What framework do we use for discerning? For those of us who are church leaders, these are particularly crucial questions. Being able to discern is vital to our work. Bernard Lonergan provides us with a valuable tool here. In all of human history, he says, there are

three basic movements: progress, decline, and redemption. When we look at any situation, any point in time, any event, one or more of these movements — several can go on simultaneously — is happening.

5. *Progress* happens when we are authentic, and to the extent that we are authentic. As you recall, authenticity is living in fidelity to the dynamism of consciousness, both within ourselves and in the world around us. It means that people, as individuals and as communities, take responsibility for the world they've constructed. They realize that it's up to them to try to make their world conform to God's will. What do we look like when we are authentic? We are using the four capacities. We are attentive to new situations, ask questions about them, make judgments about them, and then act on our judgments. And we keep doing this, because it's an ongoing process, based on ever-new experiences and situations. There's no point at which we can say, "All right. I've decided what's important about this and now I don't have to think about it again." When we are authentic, we can't help but learn, change, and grow, because this is the inevitable outcome of responding to our inner dynamism. It is a self-correcting process, always leading us on. This is when progress occurs.

6. But human beings are not perfect. We are not always authentic, not always true to our best selves. When we are not faithful to the dynamism, the process breaks down. Then we stop moving forward and actually move back. Lonergan calls this "decline." The breakdown can happen anywhere in the process and can involve any one of the capacities. Perhaps a community has constructed a shared meaning that excludes some

important information. So its members pay attention to the wrong things. Perhaps people become complacent with their horizon; they accept the status quo. So they don't ask any questions. Or maybe they do ask questions but fear stops them from forming new judgments. Or they never make decisions on their judgments. When we stop paying attention to, and stop being responsive to, the dynamism of consciousness, we stop growing. We no longer honor the inner drive that pushes us to truth and love and to God. We are inauthentic, which sometimes leads to sin. We know all too well that sin has always been part of human history and is still a part of our world. We have only to look around us to recognize it. And sin leads to decline, both in individuals and in communities.

7. But there is a counterbalance to sin: *redemption* is also always present in human history. Redemption is the solution to the problem of sin and evil. It is the supernatural aspect of our world, when God steps in and intervenes in our lives. We know that God does this; Scripture, in fact, is the record of God acting in history. God is constantly, through the Holy Spirit, offering us love and the grace to accept it. When we do accept it, we experience conversion. Our minds and hearts are reoriented, different. We are changed — willingly so — and we find that we are enabled to effect change in the world around us as well. This is redemption. It helps us be authentic and move forward again. It arrests decline.

8. It would be easy to say that God gives us redemption and we merely need to go along with it. It is, of course, true that God is the one who initiates it and that only God can offer us redemption. We don't redeem

ourselves. But we human beings do play a part in the process. We need to cooperate with the grace of the Holy Spirit that is offered — that's the first step — and then respond to it, out of love. And our response involves our whole selves, physical, mental, emotional, and spiritual, because redemption involves our whole selves. It doesn't affect us only when we pray or when we go to church, but all the time and in all situations. It involves all our basic human capacities, the ones we've been discussing.

9. Redemption also helps us grow in, and is marked by, the three virtues Paul lists in his famous hymn to love in 2 Corinthians: faith, hope, and charity. Redemption teaches us faith. We come to believe that we live in a friendly universe and that the truth is attainable. Redemption teaches us hope. We dare to think that power and violence will not win in the end. Redemption teaches us charity. We learn to love God as a friend and we find we are capable of a self-sacrificing love for others. It is this self-sacrificing love that can break the cycle of hatred and violence by absorbing it.

> We don't have to look too far to find examples of this self-sacrificing love in the world around us. One example from our recent history is the civil rights movement in this country. It began in the late 1950s, when religious leaders from the South joined forces to fight against the racism and segregation that prevailed at the time. It was a struggle of epic proportions. After all, only about forty years ago, black people in the South were lynched for stepping outside their assigned place — and this was tolerated, even condoned. But despite

the potential for the oppressed to retaliate in kind, to respond with hatred and violence, the civil rights movement was firmly based in nonviolence. Led by Dr. Martin Luther King Jr., it met with nonviolent resistance angry mobs, abusive police, and racist judges and lawmakers. It took courage, patience, commitment, and faith. It took self-sacrificing love. But in the end the movement brought together people from all over the country, black and white, oppressed and outsiders, and changed the face of our society.

A contemporary example of this kind of love is seen in the work of Médecins Sans Frontières, known in this country as Doctors Without Borders. Founded in Paris by a small group of French doctors in 1971, it is now the world's largest independent international medical relief agency, sending more than two thousand volunteers to some eighty countries every year. These doctors and other medical workers help victims of wars, epidemics, and natural and man-made disasters wherever they occur. Its members have worked in Nicaragua during an earthquake, in the civil war in Lebanon, in Afghanistan during the Soviet invasion, in Somalia during a drought, in Burundi and Rwanda during the civil war and genocide there — the list goes on and on. The organization is committed to offering emergency assistance wherever it is needed, particularly to the "forgotten populations" of the world. It also, when necessary, speaks out against human rights abuses. The members routinely face hardship and danger in the course of their work. In recognition of its commitment, Médecins Sans Frontières was awarded the Nobel Peace Prize in 1999.

10. As leaders, one of our primary tasks is to look at the world around us and try to recognize authenticity and inauthenticity as they occur. We can't always see progress or decline as they happen; we can only recognize them afterward, when we look back. Our job here and now is to discern where we, and other people and our communities, are being authentic or inauthentic, and try to facilitate the first and avoid the second. We also need to cooperate with the grace of the Holy Spirit as it is offered to us to help us in this effort. In any situation or event, we ask, "Where do I see people being authentic? Where do I see them being inauthentic? Where is the Holy Spirit at work?" Posing these questions, and trying to answer them, allows us to move beyond the common error of seeing everything simply in terms of good versus bad. All too often, this is how we look at the past; we see history as only black and white. And we tend to see the present — our world, the here and now — this way as well. We need instead to use the measuring stick of authenticity and the lens of progress, decline, and redemption as a means of helping us in our discerning.

11. It is important to realize that we can discern authenticity and inauthenticity in the world around us only if we also can discern them within ourselves. They are both constantly at work in us, just as they are at work in the world. It is our responsibility to be just as honest and just as discerning with ourselves as we are with others.

IV. Exercise: Meditation on the Trinity, the Annunciation, and the Incarnation (20 minutes)

1. Tell the participants that you will all be doing a meditation now. Explain that they have worked with the meditation over the past week, but that now you are going to do it as a group meditation. Ask people to get comfortable.

2. When everyone is quiet, read the meditation, which begins on the next page, out loud.

3. Afterward, have people share their responses to the meditation.

Note: The following meditation is based on a meditation in the *Spiritual Exercises* of Ignatius. If you want to look at the original meditation, see Joseph Tetlow's book, *Ignatius Loyola: Spiritual Exercises.* The heart of the meditation is reflecting on the decision made by the Trinity for God to join humanity. The pictures are meant to stimulate your thinking and your prayer. The first three pictures depict what the Trinity saw looking across time and space, which led to the Incarnation. The fourth picture is of Mary, who is part of that decision. You are not limited to these pictures; if you have others you wish to use, feel free to do so.

Meditation:
The Trinity, the Annunciation,
and the Incarnation

We start by seeing a secret place,
a place that is nowhere
we have ever been.
It is not on this earth;
it was before the earth was made.
It is this moment and every moment.
It was before time began
and before the universe existed.
It is now and forever.

From this place where matter is not
and this time where time is not,
the Trinity looks at the earth.
The Trinity looks at the people of the earth.
The Trinity sees all the men and women
who have ever lived,
since the world was made.

stephen a. titra

stephen a. titra

stephen a. titra

stephen a. titra

In this place sits the Trinity:
God the Father, God the Son,
God the Holy Spirit.
God creates.
God saves.
God sanctifies.
All this because God loves.
The Trinity is one in love.
The Trinity *is* love.

ANNUNCIATION

Were others asked?

A lassie from an isle in a distant sea?
A maiden in North Africa
or a slave girl from the Congo?
How many times were angels sent
and returned, unheard, unheeded?
Was Mary tenth on salvation's list,
or the hundredth?

And you, my soul,
was "fiat" spoken
when the angel came?

—Robert F. Morneau

V. Looking Ahead to Session Five (5 minutes)

1. The participants' first assignment for the next session is to read Acts 11:1–18. Ask them to keep the following questions in mind as they read: Why are the people in Jerusalem — the Jewish followers of Jesus — so upset? Why do they berate Peter for eating with Gentiles? Is that all it is, or is there more behind this objection? Can you understand their point of view? Why, after listening to Peter, do they end up accepting what he has done?

2. The second assignment is for people to answer the question: What are the obstacles we human beings face, both as individuals and as community, as we try to be authentic? In other words, what prevents us from being attentive? What prevents us from asking questions and collecting information? What stops us from making good judgments? From taking responsible action? Participants should list everything they think of. They can include obstacles they are aware of within themselves, those they have noticed in other people and in communities, and those they perceive in history. Tell them to be concrete.

3. Finally, ask people to read the article on habits in their Participant's Book (pages 79–82).

VI. Closing Prayer

Lead the group in a short closing prayer, or ask a member of the group to do it.

Note: The following material is background for the group's discussion of Acts 11:1–18, which you will lead next week.

ACTS 11:1–18: STAGES OF A CHURCH DECISION

What do you think the reaction of the folks back in Jerusalem is when they hear about all that's happened in Caesarea? They get very upset.

Now the apostles and the believers who were in Judea heard that the Gentiles had also accepted the word of God. So when Peter went up to Jerusalem, the circumcised believers criticized him, saying, "Why did you go to uncircumcised men and eat with them?"

So Peter has to explain his actions and defend himself to the community. But notice that he had companions with him when the incident in question happened, so his act of ordering baptism is already a communal act. Then he goes over the events step by step, explaining to the believers in Jerusalem his thoughts and actions, and also what God revealed to him. When he is done, all those who had criticized Peter were silenced: "When they heard this, they were silenced. And they praised God, saying, 'Then God has given even to the Gentiles the repentance that leads to life.'"

So the elders of Jerusalem seem to accept the action of Peter. Peter has been able to share his insight with them in such a way that they understand it — quite an accomplishment, when you think about it. Yet change is never this easy, especially not a change this drastic and this far-reaching. It is true that the elders have received an insight and made a judgment, but this is only the beginning of making a change. A lot more has to happen. They have to be prepared to make a decision based on their new knowledge, a decision to either follow it or reject it. They really don't understand the implications of all this; they may even think that this is an isolated instance and that they would not have to deal with pagans anymore.

Being Responsible

I. Welcome and Opening Prayer (10 minutes)

II. Processing Assignments and Scripture (20 minutes)

1. Ask people how they did with their assignment to list obstacles to being authentic. What did they think about it? Was it hard to do, or easy? Then ask what obstacles they came up with. Write them on a sheet of newsprint. Did different people come up with many of the same obstacles, and if so, what are they? Why might these same things be appearing repeatedly? Finally, ask if anyone gained any new insights by doing this exercise.

2. Have one person read out loud Acts 11:1–18. Talk about this passage. Why are the Jewish believers in Jesus so perturbed that Gentiles are also coming to believe? Why does Peter, in responding to those who are criticizing him, not just explain his reasons? Why does he tell the whole story all over again? As group members discuss the passage, write down their responses on newsprint.

III. Presentation: Being Responsible (10 minutes)

1. Transition: Point out, if this hasn't already come up in the discussion, that Peter does not immediately go on the

defensive when his actions are criticized. He doesn't just say, "I decided to do this and here's why and I'm right." He relates the story once again — how he had a vision, what the voice told him, what he said, the message from Cornelius, etc. He goes back over the whole process by which he arrived at his decision and is reflecting on the process as he does so.

2. This kind of reflection is critical to the fourth capacity of the dynamism of human consciousness — the one we have called "being responsible." Being responsible, in this context, means making authentic decisions and taking the correct action. We might ask, then, how reflection fits in, since we usually view reflection and action as opposites. Yet in order to take the correct action, in order to make good decisions, we need to look back over how we have used the other three capacities. The question that we should ask ourselves is not simply, "What do I do?" but "What should I do, now that I have been attentive to my experience, now that I have understood it, and now that I have judged that my understanding is correct?" Authentic decisions and action require that we do this looping back through the process, which actually is not a vertical movement (first this step, then this one) but more of a spiral, where we move deeper into it each time we go back over it. Action, in the sense in which we use it here, springs from, and is inextricably tied to, this kind of ongoing reflection. It means both making a decision and acting on it. All this forms the capacity that we call being responsible.

3. Putting it this way actually expands the description. Being responsible encompasses reflection, decision,

and action. It is not action taken impulsively or thought-lessly; nor is it action done in isolation. By the same token, being responsible is not just reflection by itself; it needs decision and action in order to be complete.

4. We can recognize in this capacity of being responsible connections to the fifth step of Ignatius's Examen. In this final step, we plan how we can collaborate more effectively with God as he works in our life. We resolve to make whatever changes we have discerned to be necessary as a result of doing the Examen. This is a very concrete thing. We do not make nebulous plans to reform but decide specifically what we will, with God's grace, do tomorrow, next week, next month, and so on.

5. Again, it is important to remember that being respon-sible (like the other three capacities) is not merely an individual thing but a communal thing. We live in com-munity. There is almost nothing that we know or do that is totally independent of other people. Commu-nity is grounded in shared meaning. It means we have a common field of experience (what we pay attention to), common ways of understanding (the questions we ask), common judgments (the conclusions we reach), and, finally, common principles and commitments (the decisions and actions we take).

6. When we take action — when we are being respon-sible — we are weighing our principles. We are asking ourselves, what would happen if we do this particular thing? What would be gained? What would be lost? How do we feel about these gains and these losses? Are there things we are not willing to lose? Are there things that are less important to us? In other words, what do we value most? We make our choices based on these principles.

All people, of all cultures and beliefs, engage in this process. It's a human process and is the same for everyone. But the content — what we value most — differs. For the Christian, the true measure, the deepest value, is Jesus.

7. This process of judging principles is different from, and goes beyond, making judgments of fact. When we make judgments of fact, we have to weigh evidence. When we make judgments of principle, we are using our inherent, God-given capacity to assess the true worth of things. Yet, as with everything else, we acquire our principles largely by learning them from others and from our environment — our culture, our faith, and so on. The Church, the Christian community, has the crucial task of handing on principles and of teaching us what they mean. The Church instructs us in what is good and helps form us so we may respond to the good.

Fiddler on the Roof is the story of the struggle of a man going through this process of taking action, of making responsible decisions. Tevye lives in a small village in Russia toward the end of the nineteenth century. He is poor, as are most of the other Jews in the village. They must work hard just to survive, while surrounding them lies the constant danger of a world hostile to Jews. What sustains them is their faith, and the traditions attached to it. But then Tevye's oldest daughter, Tzeitel, goes against these traditions by announcing that she can't marry the man her parents chose for her but loves another man. "Impossible! Absurd!" thinks Tevye. "The parents arrange the marriage.... But on the other hand, look at her eyes. She's happy.... On the other hand, he's a poor tailor. She'll have nothing, and she's refusing a rich husband.... On the other hand, she loves him." Tevye finally decides to allow this unconventional marriage. His daughter's happiness is more important to him than the tradition.

Then Tevye's second daughter, Hodel, tells him that she loves Perchik, a student visiting from Kiev. Perchik has radical ideas and wants to fight against the injustice all around them. "No!" says Tevye. "I will not give my permission!" "But Papa," says Hodel, "we are not asking your permission. We are going to get married. But we would like your blessing." "Impossible! Unthinkable!" thinks Tevye. "The daughter has decided herself, without the parents or a matchmaker.... On the other hand, look at her eyes. She's happy.... On the other hand, who knows what kind of life she'll have, following this dreamer around.... On the other hand, she loves him." Tevye gives the two of them his blessing, commenting that, after all, Adam and Eve had the same matchmaker they did: God. He values Hodel's happiness more than convention.

Finally, his third daughter, Chava, tries to introduce him to Fyedka — a Christian. Tevye is barely civil to him. When Chava tells him she wants to marry Fyedka, her father cuts her off, refusing to listen. So Chava and Fyedka elope, and Tevye says, "My daughter is dead." Chava comes to him and tries to explain to him why she did it, asking for acceptance if not for blessing. "Impossible!" thinks Tevye. "Can I deny everything I believe in?...On the other hand, can I deny my daughter?...On the other hand, can I deny my faith?...On the other hand...No! There is no other hand!" Tevye walks away from Chava. He cannot accept something that goes so much against his religion. That is what he values most, for it is life to him.

But later, Tevye acts again. He and all the other Jews in the village must leave their homes, forced out by the czar's orders. Tevye and his family will go to America. As they pack the few belongings they can take with them, Chava and Fyedka come and tell Tevye that they are leaving too, that they cannot stay in a place where people treat other people in this way. They will go to Krakow. Tevye does not respond. But as the young couple walk away, Tevye finally says to them, "Good-bye, and may God go with you." These few words are earth-shattering, and everyone knows it: Tevye has given his blessing. And we know that it is not because he has denied his faith but that he has somehow managed to hold both values — his faith and his love for his daughter — close to him, despite the tension between them.

IV. Exercise: Obstacles to Authenticity (20 minutes)

1. This exercise will explore more deeply the assignment participants did for this session, where they listed obstacles to being authentic. The group has already talked about the obstacles earlier in the session, but now they will be analyzing them from a different perspective.

2. On one sheet of newsprint, write at the top the word "Individual." On a second sheet, write "Structural: Fearfulness." On a third sheet, write "Structural: Institutions." On a fourth sheet, write "Structural: Impulsiveness."

3. Explain that obstacles can be either within ourselves (personal, individual obstacles) or within our community (structural obstacles). Structural obstacles are broader and more general than individual obstacles. However, the two are closely related, since our individual obstacles often are rooted in, and are a function of, our community. For this exercise, we will look at individual obstacles and three types of structural obstacles: fearfulness, institutional, and impulsiveness.

4. We see obstacles of fearfulness in such things as fear of change, fear of exclusion, fear of making mistakes, fear of loss of control, and so on. Notice that these are all fears that individuals have, but they are ones that can take root and spread in groups of people, and take on lives of their own. Many examples of fearfulness can be found in the Scriptures.

5. Institutional obstacles arise from the fact that structured institutional relationships sometimes work to prevent people from being authentic. One example of this would be a lack of healthy accountability and evaluation. Another would be a lack of adequate communication among members in a community — so decisions are made based on incomplete information.

6. Obstacles of impulsiveness have to do with not doing the necessary research to make a decision, or assuming that research doesn't even have to be done. It means not basing our decisions on facts or not letting ideas mature.

7. Point out that these obstacles can be related to any of the four human capacities — being attentive, exploring, discerning, or being responsible — but the end result is always the same. They keep us from being authentic and therefore keep us from developing gospel-based communities.

8. Now, ask people to think about the obstacles they had come up with earlier, and try to figure out which category each one belongs in. Write each obstacle on the appropriate sheet of newsprint. Does it make a difference what kind of obstacle each one is? How? Does it influence how we might approach the task of overcoming it?

9. Lastly, ask the group to choose one obstacle from each category and then discuss possible strategies for overcoming it.

V. Looking Ahead to Session Six (5 minutes)

1. For the next session, ask people to read Acts 15:1– 23, 28–29. As they read, they should keep in mind these questions: What is at stake in this controversy in the early church? Why is it significant? What obstacles to growth and authenticity do you see? How are they overcome?

2. Another assignment is for people to redraw their horizons. The instructions are the same as the first time they did it, but they should pay attention to any changes that may have occurred as a result of this seminar. Ask people to bring their redrawn horizons to the next meeting.

3. Ask people to read "The Meaning of Community" in their Participant's Book (pages 88–92).

4. Finally, you — the Facilitator — will have, before this session, identified some issue or problem. It can be something currently facing your faith community; it may well have surfaced during these sessions. Describe it to the group members, and ask them to think about this issue over the next week. Say something like:

> *Over the course of these sessions, this particular issue has come up. Let's look at it more deeply. What are your thoughts about it? What ideas do you have about it? Do you see any possible solutions? What should we do and how? Now, in doing*

this, remember that this isn't a perfect world, and we know that we're not a perfect community. Don't be sidetracked by issues like church structures. We will explore this issue, and your thoughts on it, at the next session.

VI. Closing Prayer (5 minutes)

Ask one member of the group to lead all of you in a final prayer.

Note: This material is background for you about this passage. The group will not be discussing it next week, but we suggest you use it as a reading during the Eucharist.

ACTS 15:1–23, 28–29: A CHURCH DECISION

While Peter was baptizing Gentiles in Caesarea, Paul and Barnabas had been sent out to bring the good news of Jesus to the Jewish people in Antioch and other places outside Jerusalem. They encountered strong resistance and even attacks from some of them but also discovered that many Gentiles were responding to their words. Again, Paul and Barnabas were content to admit the Gentiles into the Church without too much ado, but then we read in chapter 15:

Then certain individuals came down from Judea and were teaching the brothers, "Unless you are circumcised according to the custom of Moses, you cannot be saved." And after Paul and Barnabas had no small dissension and debate with them, Paul and Barnabas and some of the others were appointed to go up to Jerusalem to discuss this question with the apostles and the elders. So they were sent on their way by the church, and as they passed through both Phoenicia and Samaria, they reported the conversion of the Gentiles, and brought great joy to all the believers. When they came to Jerusalem, they were welcomed by the church and the apostles and the elders, and they reported all that God had done with them. But some believers who belonged to the sect of the Pharisees stood up and said, "It is necessary for them to be circumcised and ordered to keep the law of Moses."

What is at stake here? At stake is the self-understanding of the Church. Is it a Jewish reform movement, is it just another Jewish sect, or is it something else? Obviously the Pharisee believers wanted this new community to become a reform movement within Judaism and nothing more. Thus, they would insist that the Gentiles, if they wished to belong, had to in effect become Jewish.

Peter, who already had the experience of a real change of perspective in his dealing with Cornelius, takes the lead and addresses the assembled leaders:

The apostles and the elders met together to consider this matter. After there had been much debate, Peter stood up and said to them, "My brothers, you know that in the early days God made a choice among you, that I should be the one through whom the Gentiles would hear the message of the good news and become believers. And God, who knows the human heart, testified to them by giving them the Holy Spirit, just as he did to us; and in cleansing their hearts by faith he has made no distinction between them and us. Now therefore why are you putting God to the test by placing on the neck of the disciples a yoke that neither our ancestors nor we have been able to bear? On the contrary, we believe that we will be saved through the grace of the Lord Jesus, just as they will."

The whole assembly kept silence, and listened to Barnabas and Paul as they told of all the signs and wonders that God had done through them among the Gentiles.

Now it is time for the whole Church to be converted, for the whole Church to understand itself and its mission differently, to understand that they are not just to be another Jewish sect but a gathering place of all humans, regardless of their religious or cultural background. James, who is the one who makes official pronouncements as leader of the Church in Jerusalem, makes the official decision.

After they finished speaking, James replied, "My brothers, listen to me. Simeon has related how God first looked favorably on the Gentiles, to take from among them a people for his name.... Therefore I have reached the decision that we should not trouble those Gentiles who are turning to God, but we should write to them to abstain only from things polluted by idols and from fornication and from whatever has been strangled and from blood." Then the apostles and the elders, with the consent of the whole church, decided to choose men from among their members and to send them to Antioch with Paul and Barnabas. They sent Judas called Barsabbas, and Silas, leaders among the brothers, with the following letter: "The brothers, both the apostles and the elders, to the believers of Gentile origin in Antioch and Syria and Cilicia, greetings. Since we have heard that certain persons who have gone out from us, though with no instructions from us, have said things to disturb you and have unsettled your minds, we have decided unanimously to choose representatives and send them to you, along with our beloved Barnabas and Paul, who have risked their lives for the sake of our Lord Jesus Christ. We have therefore sent Judas and Silas, who themselves will tell you the same things by word of mouth. For it has seemed good to the Holy Spirit and to us to impose on you no further burden than these essentials: that you abstain from what has been sacrificed to idols and from blood and from what is strangled and from fornication. If you keep yourselves from these, you will do well. Farewell."

What was the significance of this decision? We now understand that the Church of Jesus was not to be a reform movement within Judaism but rather that its mission was nothing less than the transformation of all humanity.

Many believe that God is still pushing the edges of the envelope and constantly calling us to become more inclusive, more open to others, to different peoples, to new cultures. But there will continue to be resistance, ill feeling, and mistakes made, so we should not be surprised that we still have divisions among well-meaning Catholics.

Session Six

Community

Note: Members should have brought their redrawn horizons with them. Ask for them as people arrive, explaining that you want to put them up on the wall around the room. This helps create a learning environment; the horizons show the changes that have taken place in the group members.

I. Welcome and Opening Prayer (5 minutes)

II. Exercise: Exploring an Issue within Community (30 minutes)

1. Now is the time for the group to examine the particular issue or problem that you assigned them at the last meeting. Approach this as a brainstorming session. Put up sheets of newsprint on the wall, and ask people for their thoughts and ideas. Write them on the sheets, without comment. This is not the time for anyone to object or criticize or even analyze. Don't get sidetracked by stopping to look at the merits or problems of a suggestion. The goal is to come up with as many creative thoughts as possible, and you do this by letting people build on each other's ideas.

2. What happens next will depend on you and your group. An obvious direction may show itself, a course of action that seems to beg to be pursued. It may be that your

group realizes that they do not agree on exactly what the problem is — but this is progress, too. Or the group may decide that several ideas are worth pursuing, or that nothing clear was determined but the process is a good one and should be continued. It is important to remember that you are not trying to come up with solutions now. You are working together, as a community within a community, to follow God's will for you.

III. Eucharist (45 minutes)

1. We suggest you use Acts 15:1–23, 28–29 (or a portion of it) for the first reading and the story of the Annunciation in Luke for the Gospel (1:26–38).

2. Celebrate the Eucharist. Try to involve everyone in the group, as readers, eucharistic ministers, gift bearers, and so on.

3. At the offertory, the celebrant may say something like the following:

> *You have spent time with each other and with God, trying to grow as individuals and as church leaders within our community. You have studied together, prayed together, and shared together. You have learned a great deal about yourselves and about each other. You have come to understand how important you are to each other and to our community. You all have gifts, talents, and abilities. Now, if you wish, you may say a few words about what you hope to offer our community in its ongoing journey toward God.*

Follow-up: We suggest that the group come together again after some time has passed — perhaps two or three months. Meet to explore some issue of importance to your community. See if the Ignatian-Lonergan method of making decisions that you learned in these sessions can be applied to this issue.